A Poetry

by

Ana Sigmaringen

Table of Contents

Foreword

When I set out to write the following book of poetry, it was with a heavy heart. We had lost our little girl just minutes after birth, and the heartache and sorrow was deeper than we ever could have imagined.

A few weeks later, we began talking about all the things we would never get to do with her, all of the memories we would never make, and it was then that we discovered the reborn movement. Not to say that anyone or anything could ever replace our little girl, because nothing ever will, nothing could even come close, but adopting a reborn allowed us to feel the comfort of holding a baby, and feel like our love could be directed somewhere rather than simply into the ether.

There are a lot of reasons for reborn parents to love their babies, and in all different walks of life. Perhaps you are a collector, a creator of these babies, know an Alzheimer's patient that finds comfort in them, or just love them simply because holding a lifelike baby is a wonderful way to relax and make a compassionate connection. Yes, there are always critics, and not everyone will understand, but that doesn't matter to those of us who are truly dedicated to these little ones.

I hope that you enjoy the following poems, and that you can relate to them. May you always find peace and happiness with those you love, born, or reborn.

2016

Dedicated to Sharina Evangeline, our beautiful butterfly.

Resting Like an Angel

When I look into your face
My cherubic dream come true
As you drift to sleep in my arms
Nothing else matters but you.

The world stops spinning
There is no day or night
Only your radiance
Everything is right.

Tiny hands
Perfect toes
A child created just for me
You fill my heart with
More joy and warmth
Than I could have believed.

Sleep my precious angel
Dream away all your fears
And wake in the safety
Of my embrace
As I hold you near.

I Remember

I remember the first time

I looked into your tiny face

An immediate connection

Beyond time or space.

Your gentle baby lips

So soft against my skin

A feeling indescribable

Poured out from within.

I dreamt of you before

You became reality

My special soul companion

The other half of me.

What I See

What I see when I look at you

Is something heavenly,

Divine

I am so lucky to have you

To know that you are

Mine

I cuddle you against me

Your small body against my own

The sweetest moment

We do share

Such love I've never known

Perhaps

Perhaps to others you

Are just a doll

An object or a thing

But to me you are the epitome

Of everything I need

You want nothing from me

But my love and tender care

And every time I look at you

I know there's someone there

Perhaps not from my womb

Not nine months and then a birth

But the day you came into my life

You changed my world, my earth

I don't care what they say

The whispers of passersby

You mean so much to me

You complete my life

You Will

You will never grow up

To be a toddler child

Or play like others do

Riding bikes and running wild

You will not attend a proper school

Go to prom or university

You may not grow old and grey

But that matters not to me

You will not ever

Long for my embrace

And I will not need photos

To remind me of your youthful face

You will be here by my side

And I will love you just as much

As years pass us by

You will always feel my touch

You will not outgrow your clothes

Or the toys that you have loved

But angels are eternal

When they come from above

Our Day

I can't wait to see you every morning

When I dress you for your day

I love taking care of you

More than words can say

Itty bitty sockies

And clothes so delicate

The things I find when we are out

I can't resist but get

You lying there so quietly

With your teddy in your arms

How could anyone possibly

Be immune to your charms?

The way your toes curl in

And your fingers fall into fists

The way you smile so sleepily

My eyes begin to mist

I hope others find such joy

With a baby against their chest

Settling in the evening

Slipping into beautiful rest

Under the Christmas Tree

A rocking horse so shiny
As you smile from ear to ear
Pictures with lights twinkling
Decked out in Christmas gear

Strings of popcorn make you curious
You reach for everything
The pretty ribbons
And gingerbread house
Filled with jeweled candy

I want you to experience
The joy and festive season
And buying you pretty presents...
It gives me a good reason

Christmas is for children
Of all races, ages, size
And I marvel at your wonder
And the excitement in your eyes

Don't you worry baby

Santa loves you, true

All the newborn babies

And the reborns too

Before

Before you came into my life

There was a void I could not fill

No matter what I did in life

I felt that hollow still

The first time I saw you

I knew what I was missing

It was your love, your light

The times we'd spend

Just hugging and kissing

You put me on a new path

One filled with love and laughter

Never to be empty again

Now full forever after

Everything

The clouds

The sky

A butterfly

The sea

A shell

A wishing well

A bee

A flower

The twilight hour

The morning sun

A breezy day

An eagle swooping

Above the bay

All the things

I want to show you

All the places we will go

My companion in exploration

What is next?

Who knows?

Magic

You make some kind of magic
That lives inside of us
I love watching you with daddy
He holds you when you fuss

And when sit down
In the field, beneath a starry sky
I am startled by the immensity
Of love that within me lie

You have got his nose,
His cheeks
And my eyes

You have got my hair
My fingers
And daddy's smile

You came to us a different way
Than most would understand
But to us you are the fairest princess
That ever lived in any land

The Day

The day you were delivered

By post rather than pain

I sat beside the window

Looking expectantly all day

I just knew that I would adore you

And you were meant to be my love

A gift of divine proportions

Sent from the Lord above

Some might not understand

The bond that you and I share

But I love you more than life itself

And for their opinions I do not care

If they were to hold you

And let first judgments fall away

It might change their perceptions

And the cruel things they say

What's wrong with loving someone

the way that I love you?

To care and hold and appreciate

Is all I wish to do

When I was Younger

When I was a little girl
I loved my dolls so much
I pretended they were real babies
And offered them my most gentle touch

I dreamed of being a mommy
With a child to hold and rock
Making outfits out of my old clothes
And knitting little socks

I grew up and had babies,
The type that laugh and cry
I watched them grow and move away
As time quickly passed by

Then one day I found you,
In a random search online
And instantly I knew,
You had to be mine

I waited with anxiety

For you to arrive

And the first time I held you

I felt so very alive

I've raised my beautiful children

And now I'm grandma too

But I find such comfort in your embrace

And I do so love you

You are a part of my heart and soul

You and your little teddy bear

And I can find no fault in giving you

The love I have to spare

So Real

So real, people say

When they see you out with me

Some of them give odd looks

Curious as can be

I've seen them in the chat rooms

All with opinions to give

"How sad for these poor people"

"That's no way to live."

They assume that I'm imbalanced

And I have you because I can't have kids

Or because I've lost someone

But that's not what it is

I enjoy holding babies

The feeling is so sublime

There's nothing else like it

It calms me every time

Would the world not be better

if everyone had a hobby like this?

I'm too busy bathing you,

Reading bedtime stories

And sending you to sleep with a kiss

Spring

We walked together in the garden
Among the flowers in bloom
We picked a few of the bigger ones
And put them in your room

I held the flowers to your tiny nose
And let you take a sniff
You watched a butterfly overhead
You are such a special gift

We share each day together
I'm always happy to see your face
As we explore the world outdoors
And make each a special place

Daddy and you

I wasn't sure how he would take it
When I suggested we adopt
A subject we had broached before
But then the matter dropped

Both busy with careers
No time for kids, we thought
But the idea of not being parents
Left me rather distraught

I told him about you first
And then showed him your photo
I waited nervously
Not sure how it would go

He agreed that we could try it
But reminded me you were a doll
Not to get too attached
For that couldn't be healthy at all

Funny how he said that then

As I sneak around the corner

Carefully he's bathing you

And telling his daughter...

How he adores her

I smile to myself

As I see you two together

Daddy and his little girl

A bond forged

For forever

The Sweetest Things

He falls asleep on my shoulder

As to lullabies we sway

This might be my favourite time

The close of every day

Your body so soft against mine

I love your baby smell

Just like the first time I held you

How in love I fell

The moonlight filters through the window

Casting a soft illuminance

As my baby boy and I

Do the nighttime dance

The Album

There you are on your first day

Dressed carefully but mismatched

Daddy tried his hardest

He dressed you funny in the past

In this one it is Easter

You look cute in bunny ears

Sitting next to a big basket

It has been so many years

Every year we grow older

But you, darling, never change

And neither does our love for you

No matter how we age

Thank you

Thank you precious baby

For lighting my life so

For giving me a reason

to smile, to laugh, to glow

Thank you my sweet angel

For reminding me

That sometimes the smallest things

Are the most important we will see

Thank you little darling

For letting me share my love with thee

And thank you even more

For becoming such a part of me

Beeswax!

Do they know that isn't a real baby?

People ask and question.

As if we are crazy

Because of their suggestion.

No, we hadn't realised...

You mean she doesn't talk?

And all this time we were convinced

She was just saving her energy...

To learn how to walk.

What's wrong with those people?

Some folks have often asked

Those poor souls are so confused

Lyrically they waxed

Let me answer this the simplest way I can

That, there, is our daughter

And this our little man

We do not care for your opinion

Nor wish to suffer your attacks

So take care of your own children

And mind your own beeswax

Thank you so much for taking the time to download and read this book. If you enjoyed it (or even if you didn't) please take a moment and leave a review on Amazon. I really appreciate the support and your opinions help me get better at my chosen craft.

Thank you!

Manufactured by Amazon.ca
Acheson, AB

12865932R00037